SCHIRMER'S LIBRA
OF MUSICAL CLASSIC

G. CONCONE

Op. 9

Fifty Lessons for the Voice

→ For High Voice — Vol. 1468

For Medium Voice — Vol. 242

For Low Voice — Vol. 243

G. SCHIRMER, Inc.

DISTRIBUTED BY

HAL•LEONARD®
CORPORATION
7777 W. BLUEMOUND RD. P.O. BOX 13819 MILWAUKEE, WI 53213

Printed in the U. S. A.

CONCONE, GIUSEPPE, a famous Italian Master of Singing and of the Pianoforte, was born in Turin in the year 1810, where he died in June, 1861.

His musical education was had in Turin, where he continued to live until he met with discouragement on the failure of his first opera, "Un episodio di San Michel," which was performed in 1836. In 1837 he moved to Paris, where he became famous as a teacher of the pianoforte, singing, the theory of music and composition. While resident in Paris, Concone became very popular as a composer of Romanzas, Arias and Duettini; but his chief title to fame rests on a Series of Solfeggi which have a world-wide reputation and are everywhere in use—they are eminently practical and melodious, with a flowing accompaniment.

The political developments of 1848, together with fears of revolution, moved Concone to return to his native town, where he continued to reside until his death in June, 1861.

Shortly after his return he was appointed Organist of the Royal Chapel in Turin, which position he held at the time of his death.

Concone's principal published works are:

Two Operas: Un episodio di San Michel (Turin, 1836), Graziella (never performed), Five volumes of Solfeggi, consisting of Fifty Lessons, Thirty Exercises, Twenty-five Lessons, Fifteen Vocalises, Forty Lessons for Bass.

Two Masses, Sacred Music, Romanzes, Arias, Duettini.

A large number of settings of the lyrics contained in Walter Scott's Novels, published under the head of "Walter Scott Lyrique."

(C. B.)

PREFACE

The sterling value and great usefulness of Concone's lessons have been so long recognized and so generally admitted, that their extensive adoption caused, as a natural consequence, the issue of numerous editions in almost every country where the study of the Art of Singing is cultivated. No edition, however, which has hitherto come under my notice, seems to me as correct, complete, and reliable as it should be.

I have endeavored to rectify this deficiency by adding, in the present edition, signs of expression and phrasing, where I considered it expedient to do so, completing, and, in some cases, altering the breathing-marks, and altogether carefully revising the whole work.

The purpose of these lessons—in their Author's own words—is:—

    I. "To place and fix the voice accurately;"
    II. "To develop *taste* while singing broad, elegant, and rhythmical melodies."

I recommend their practice, in conjunction with the Vocal Exercises to be found in my "Method of Singing"—after the system of respiration and voice-production therein explained has been sufficiently mastered.

The first Twenty-five Lessons are intended to be sung as "*Solfeggi*"—viz., pronouncing on every note its corresponding Italian name (*Do, re, mi, fa, sol, la, si*), and emitting each tone with equality, purity, intensity of voice, and preciseness of intonation.

All these Fifty Lessons should be *vocalised*—viz., sung upon the broad and open sound of the Italian vowel A (as pronounced in the word *Father*).

ALBERTO RANDEGGER.

Fifty Lessons

For the Medium Part of the Voice

Transposed for Soprano or Tenor

Giuseppe Concone. Op. 9

Printed in the U.S.A.

Moderato assai (♩ = 92)

20

Andantino cantabile (♪= 88)

Air with Variations

sempre legato

simile

35

41

Moderato assai quasi andante (♩=72)
cantabile, legato e sostenuto

42

Allegro giusto, sempre sostenuto (♩ = 116)

D.C. al Fine

Air with Variations